PRESSURE SYSTEM

PRESSURE SYSTEM
A Field Manual for Paradox
J. A. Gucci

PRESSURE SYSTEM
© 2026 J. A. Gucci
All rights reserved.

No part of this book may be reproduced, stored in a retrieval system, or transmitted in any form or by any means—electronic, mechanical, photocopying, recording, or otherwise—without prior written permission of the author, except for brief quotations used in reviews or scholarly discussion.

This book is a work of poetry. Any resemblance to actual persons, living or dead, or actual events is incidental and unintentional.

First edition

ISBN: 979-8-9946751-0-6

Printed in the United States of America

CONTENTS

I. CONDITIONS

Hayflick
Umfeld
Cracked Shells
Ballast
Still Dangling
Kettle Lake
Snow Sheath
Playa Bloom
June Gloom
Zero Shadow Day
Iteration
Ironwood
Boom
Bread
Lee Side

II. TENSIONS

Lydian
Dotted Line
Laid Out
Long Roll
Holdfasts
Crystallography
Camera Click
Callus
Road Rash
White Smoke
Tessellation

Tavy
Infinity
Qualia
Chilling Hour
Gazpacho

III. ECHOS

Residue
Ghost Perch
Koala Plate
Chef's Kiss
Gaze
Antiseptic
Epoxy
Panhandle Hook
Box Jelly
Tennis Court

*"The structure holds.
Whether you do is not its concern."*

I. Conditions

Hayflick

Redwood on reef
spit out—
white smoker.

A battery powered sponge
exhales,
hot air—
cool ocean gurgles.

A germ
teetering dawn,
oogonia dusk,
a clock explodes—

cracked eggs.

Umfeld

A frozen tongue,
toe,

polishing—
faint trickling,

brine—
rusty river.

A mind
stuck between poles,
floating over a hole.

Smoothed over a coastline,
a circle of footprints—

I measure eternity
with a sock.

Cracked Shells

Cracked shells—
rock bed in a dry creek—
crow caw.

Mother tree feeds
a sapling sprout—
nurse log.

Moonlit boil lumbering
downslope—
grip,
flip—

cracked shells.

Ballast

A flanked ass,
heaps of hay—
three-legged stand.

A ladder
jutting a ditch,
slumped in mud—
I chat with a shadow.

A broken keel—
waft of wind—

turtled.

Still Dangling

Porcupine gaze—
pawpaw dangling—
still.

Nip-twig—
cracked bone.

Wind—
pawpaw dangling—

wobbling.

Kettle Lake

Swollen frozen cracks,
shards of slate,
a glacier plucks a rockhead.

Plodding, slogging,
scraping,
deep gaping—

rain, sun,
an ocean breeze—
a kettle lake.

Snow Sheath

Packed snow
over ice—

shoveler sheathes
a blade—

bone-jar.

Playa Bloom

Inflated flowers,
wet rock—
bloom.

Arid air,
cracked playa—

tumbleweed.

June Gloom

Swelling hull,
waves unfold
waves,
blue heeled horizon—

half the way,
a quarter,
an eighth…

Phantom islands,
whispering winds.

Zero Shadow Day

A glass fir,
shimmering nest
egg,

zero shadow day—
preen oil on cullet—

glints.

Iteration

Et cetera, et cetera,
up the schefflera I go!
The leaf is thin, the stem is green,
the space is narrow in between,
but up and up I go.

And so on, and so forth,
and henceforth, and thenceforth—
the gravity is pulling south,
the climb is tasting in my mouth,
as to the north I go.

Et cetera, et cetera,
the vine is stretching like a wire—
so on and so forth,
and henceforth and thenceforth,
into the Quarth I go…

Et cetera!

Ironwood

Ironwood—
gritty wind—
resin shadows.

Boom

Air—
clear,

cloudy—
quiescent.

Updrafts and downdrafts,
ground shadows,

a step leader—
upward streamer—
return stroke—

Bread

Flour well—
cracked eggs,

a cold kettle hisses—
roiling,
boiling,

whistling—
clock beeps…

Lee Side

Lee side tumbling,
eddies break a bluff—
bleeding crown.

Folded branch,
flat leaves—
a narrow cone
bends with a gust—

snap.

II. Tensions

Lydian

A pulse of air,
ricocheting—
conical bore.

I press a key—
two,
now three.

A broken reed—
a major scale—

raised fourth.

Dotted Line

Glass cage—
Windsor knot,
side-part.

A fresh pen—
my trembling hand—
blank dotted line.

Black box—
Windsor knot,
side-part.

Laid Out

A coat,
hat,
a cashmere sweater—
draped over a cameo.
Wrinkled tie—
folded galluses
tucked in a shoe.

I sit—
a floorboard squeaks—

dust
settles.

Long Roll

Taps—
level,
bouncing on a drum.

Swollen sheaths,
a tingling thumb—

taps—
rugged—
fluttering on drum.

Holdfasts

Holdfasts—
rounded pillows—
surge.

Gas bladders undulate,
upright rubber stipe—

drift.

Crystallography

Six-sided
desert dust—
adrift .

Arm reflects
arm, reflects
air—

dry pockets,
wet drafts—

thin needles
spawn,

flat plate—
a clump of ice.

Camera Click

A double slit—
camera click.

A memory erased—
waves.

Callus

A thousand heel strikes:
skips,
jumps—

a flexible bow,
stiff—
a fractured bone.

Road Rash

Shoved by asphalt,
sudden left lean—
straight run.

Upslope—
downshift—
a cramped leg—

hot fatty tissue.

Misread

Walnut escritoire,
faded green felt,
a well of ink—
pounce.

Dib a nib—
fluttering goose quill:
a pink kiss—
a red seal.

. . .

Broken wax,
a jug of wine—
tipped,
hollow.

A flickering wick—
embers—
white smoke.

Tessellation

A stack of daughters—
circles,
elongated ovals—

nesting…
heaping…

frayed lump—
heaping…

Tavy

Deep nectaries—
flickering tongue.

Wild custard apples
dangling,
comet orchids.

Infinity

Infinity…
shrunk—

statue—
Dorian chants,
smoke,

contained in a book,
a cup,
veil.

Silence.

Qualia

Thoughts—
twitching neuron,
a dream—
scrolling,

bitter coffee,
grief.

Chilling Hour

Alligator charring,
ghost logs—
sickly-sweet air.

Chilling hour,
red light flash,
a seed cracks—

Ember Rose.

Gazpacho

Steamy soup in a vacuum—
double glass walls.

A narrow neck—
corked,
light seepage—

III. Echoes

Residue

Brittle—
purple and porous,
dangling from a dish,
dropped in a deluge.

Swollen pulp,
plants—
pressed, plowed—
shimmering quartz counter.

Drooped in a dish,
purple and pitted—

petrified.

Ghost Perch

Owl on a limb—
poised.

A buzzing bat,
silent hornet—

ghost perch.

Koala Plate

Eucalyptus.
A flat plate.

Koala eyes—
sunken.

Chef's Kiss

Cranked—
cracked seeds,
a slopping blade.

Strained pulp gurgling,
terracotta pot,

ricotta top,
green leaf—

a crust of bread.

Gaze

Gaze…

One finger—
heater…

a wiggle—
a change-up…

fist—
high and tight…

Gaze…

Antiseptic

A broken leg—
truncated
green-black slime.

A stone—
a blind incision—
surgical fever.

Clean cuts—
shimmering floorboards—

mint breath.

Epoxy

She dances with a pothole,
sings to a speed bump,
stuck—

I pry her with a putty,
tuck her in a glove—
buff smooth,
matte—
shimmering vinyl
spot.

Sun through glass,
pale shadow—
flower pedestal
in the glare.

Panhandle Hook

Panhandle hook,
packed over frost.

Cracked slab—
a tree snaps—
plume.

Jagged air,
silence—

wind sculpted ridges.

Box Jelly

Brainless box jelly
hidden in light.

Eye clusters—
out of focus—
a mangrove.

Inflated body—
a fake giant—

sting.

Tennis Court

I measure a bag
with a tape,

an airway
with a scan,

a sac,
with a scope—

a small lung—
a tennis court.

COLOPHON

This book was set in a serif typeface chosen for clarity and restraint and printed on acid-free paper.

All poems were written by the author.

Printed in the United States.

www.ingramcontent.com/pod-product-compliance
Lightning Source LLC
LaVergne TN
LVHW041637070526
838199LV00052B/3409